# Copyright 2020

Christina & Johnnie Johnson

Library of Congress Cataloging Data is available
ISBN
Paperback: 978-1-7354233-3-3
Hardback: 978-1-7354233-4-0
eBook: 978-1-7354233-5-7

# Dedication:

We dedicate this book to our sons Christian and Elijah. We pray that this book inspires them to obey God's word and follow His will for their lives. We also pray that this book encourages them and all boys to commit to purity and to obey the word of God so that they can marry the Princess God created just for them.

I'm Christian; this is my little brother Elijah and my sister Jee-Jee. We live with our mom and my stepdad. I am thankful for my mom because she took care of me by herself until she married my stepdad.

I look up to my stepdad, and I desire to be just like him when I grow up. I call him Pops because I respect him, and I refer to him as my dad.

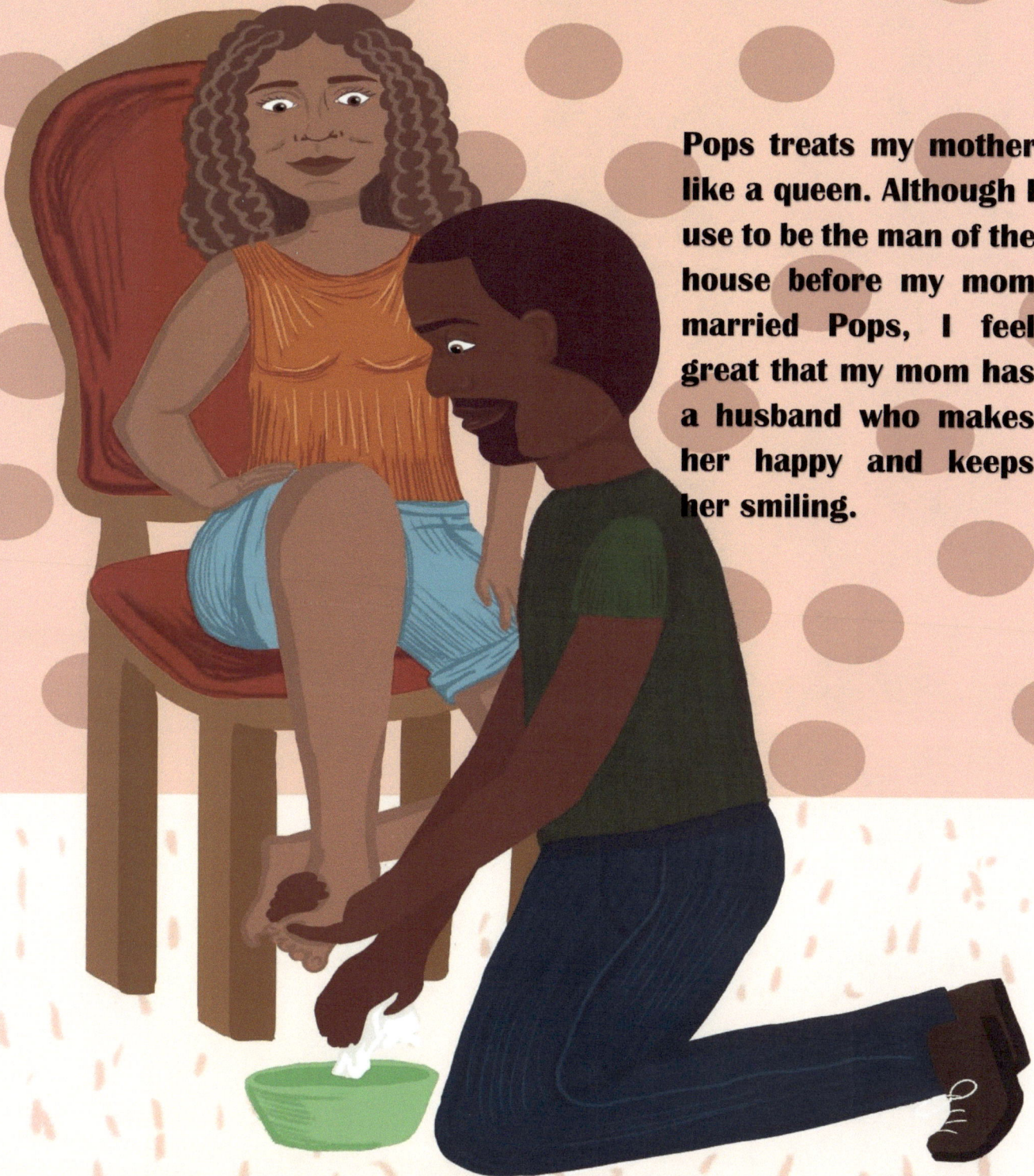

Pops treats my mother like a queen. Although I use to be the man of the house before my mom married Pops, I feel great that my mom has a husband who makes her happy and keeps her smiling.

My mom did everything as a single mother, but now she relaxes, and she watches Pops take charge.

Pops does nearly everything. He works hard, mows the lawn, washes the cars, takes out the trash, and even helps mom with laundry and cleaning the house. I love to see my mom smile as Pops opens doors for her, drives her places, and takes her out on dates. Elijah looks up and smiles hard when he sees him show affection to our mom. Pops pray with mom and all of us in the family too. He is truly an awesome man, and I want to be just like that when I grow up.

Mom and Pops help me understand that even though I had poor examples of a good man in the past, I have free will to choose to do right as a young man to grow up to be a better man.

At school and outside in my community, I've made poor choices that disappointed my mom and Pops, but they have always forgiven me and taught me about integrity. I know that I have to stand out and make wise decisions even if everyone else around me is doing wrong; I have to choose to do what is right.

Sometimes, I think my parents don't understand how difficult it can be to be an oddball. All kids want to fit in. No kid wants to be different.

Every time I got in trouble, it was doing what my peers were doing. I didn't dare to stand up, stand out, or to be different.

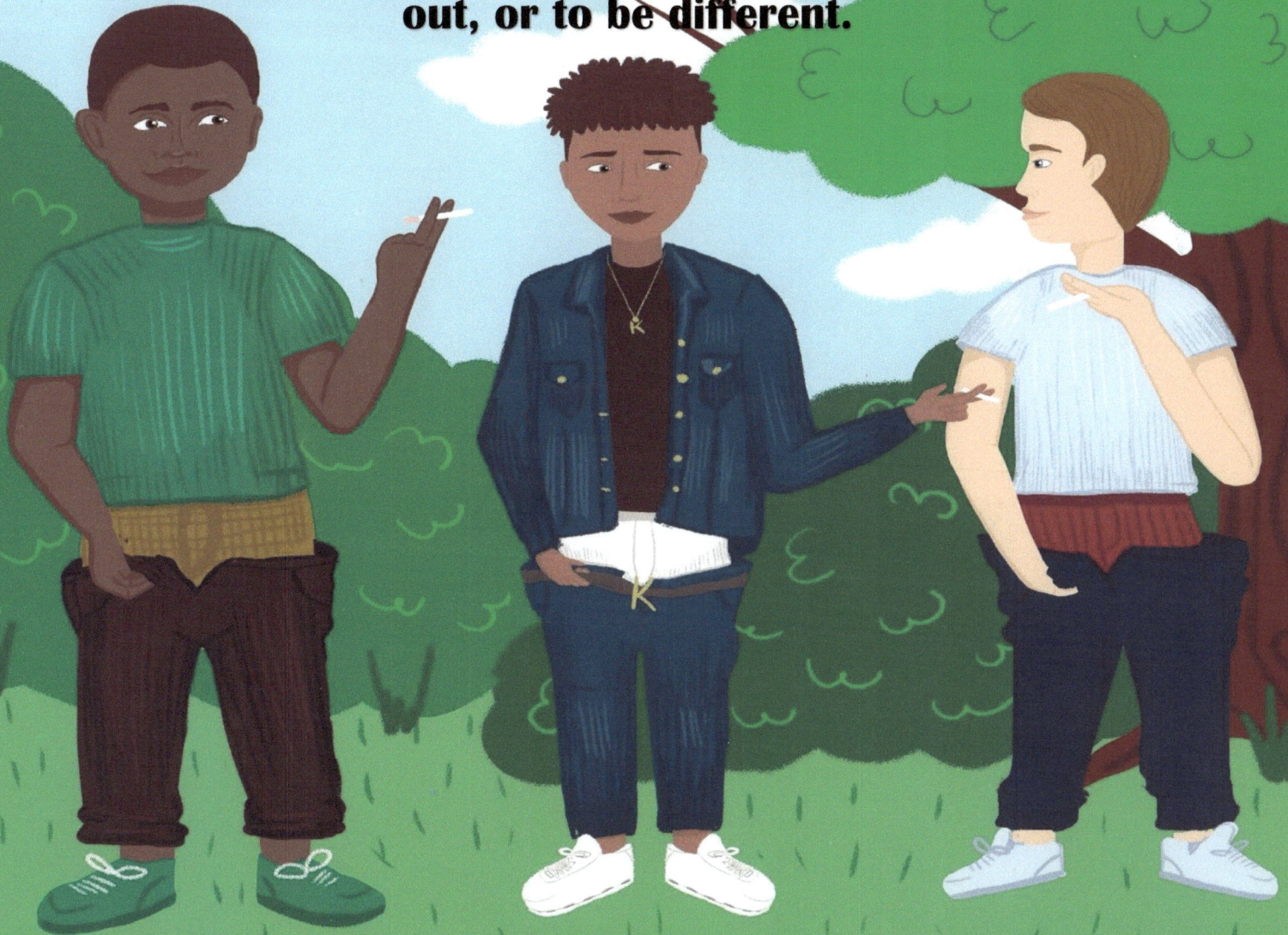

Now that I know that following negative influences can result in consequences, I have chosen to stand up and make better decisions.

Mom gives me lots of great advice, but she always says that a Godly father can teach a boy how to be a man better than a mother can.

I asked Pops to teach me what it takes to be a good guy so that I can set an excellent example for Elijah, and we can grow up to be good men just like him. I want to be a Prince and marry a Princess one day so that I can make her feel like a Queen every day and enjoy seeing her smiles filled with happiness just like Pops does to my mom.

Pops sat me down and kept it real with me. He handed me a band and asked if I could put it on my left ring finger until my Princess replaces it with a wedding band. He asked me to wear that band with honor and to vow to stay pure until I choose a princess to be my wife. He taught me how to be a young king and a Godly man.

Pops said, "first you have to know that you are a child of the highest God. God gives you free will, so you can choose to do right, or you can choose to do wrong.

Your actions display your choices, your actions become your character, and your character is your reputation in life. If you want to be known as a good man, you have to choose to act like a good man.

To be a good man, you have to put God first and follow God's lead in your life. While you are single, you must exhibit the characteristics of a Godly man. When you follow God, he will direct you to your princess; then, you must demonstrate a Godly Husband's principles. You have to follow God to lead your wife. When you and your wife choose to have children, you must exhibit the characteristics and principles of a Godly Father.

# To be A Godly man, you must:

- Make Jesus Christ Lord over your life, confess Jesus as your Lord and Savior so that you can inherit the Holy Spirit and the promises God has for you here on earth. Commit yourself to live by God's word. If things get rough, know that God shows you grace and mercy, and He will always be present with your spirit, soul, and body.

- Learn how to be yourself and not follow the crowd. A Godly man shows love not only to his loved ones but to his enemies as well. You have to walk in God's love by being patient, kind, and understanding; not judgmental but transparent. Be a leader so that the younger boys can look up to you. Great leaders don't follow the crowd; they stand out.

- Be willing to do what is right in every situation, even if everyone else is doing wrong. Doing right is leaning on what God says in His Word.

- You have to be a man of prayer and stay in daily communication with God so He can lead you to be a blessing and a leader for those connected to you in your life.

- Do not submit to Satan, the less of the flesh or things of the world, but you must daily submit your will to Jesus Christ to resist the devil and temptations that might come against you.

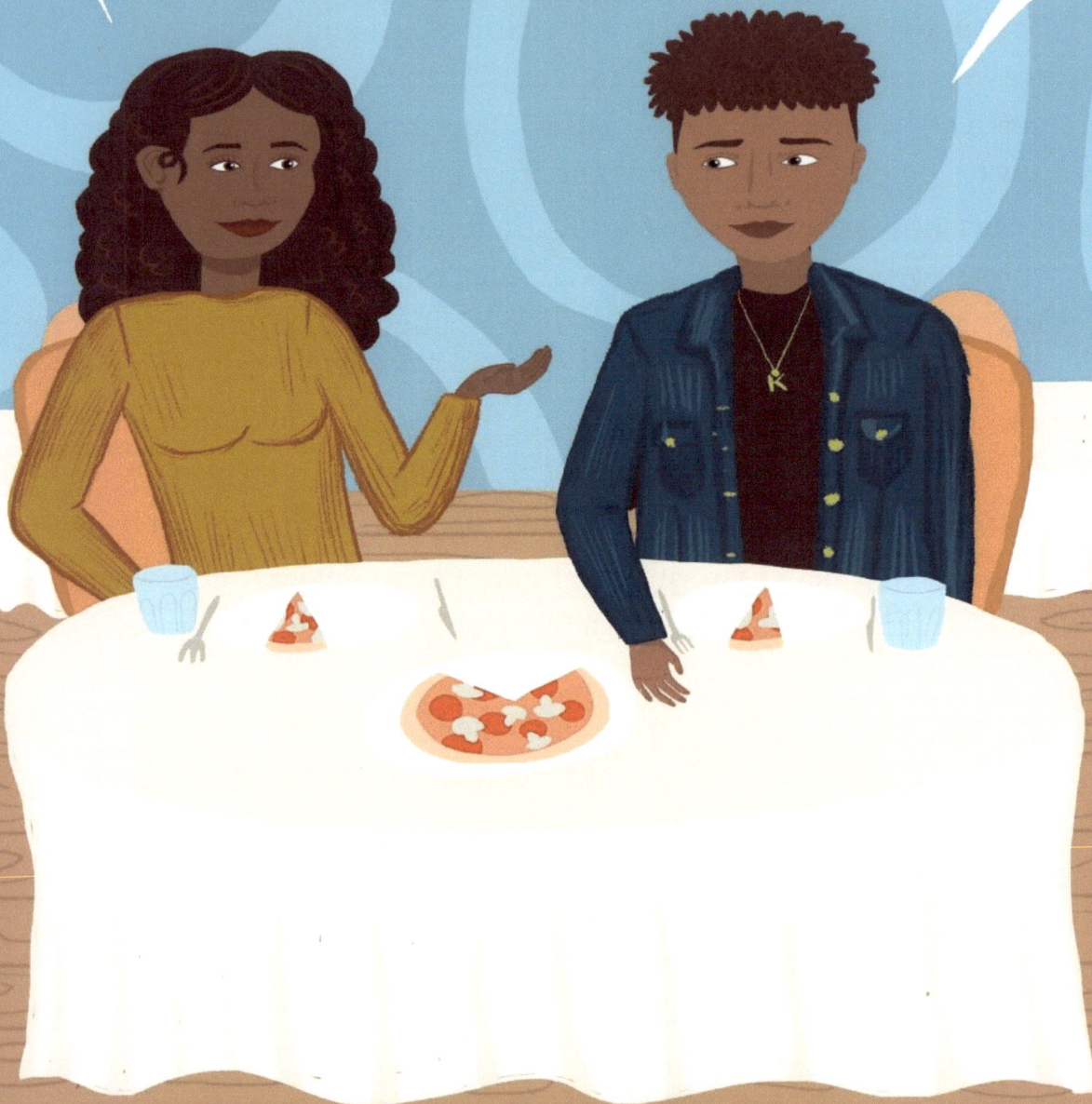

- Seek forgiveness for your past mistakes and choose to make wise decisions for your life. Do this by remaining pure until you marry "the one" God is preparing for you.

- Ignore the misconceptions that guys have to "get it" or have a certain number. When you vow to purity, you choose to respect yourself and respect the women you choose to date. Your relationships should remain innocent, filled with talks, games, fun, and laughter. You must refrain from any actions that are not pleasing to God.

- Get to know the heart of a woman to find true love. Her heart holds the characteristics of who she is. You have to see her from the inside out. You must get to know ladies, one at a time, until God tells you that she is "the one" for you. When you acknowledge "the one," your courtship should last at least a year, while pure, then you should propose to her. If you feel you cannot exhibit self-control, then give a marriage proposal right away so that you do not give in to temptation before your special day. When you choose to follow that order and then go before God, you'll become Prince, and then God will grant you and your princess a blessed marriage forever on your wedding day.

# To be a Godly husband, you must:

- Be willing to put your wife's needs before your needs and wants. You have to sacrifice your time, talent, and desires for her.
- You have to be willing to take a risk and be uncomfortable to make sure your family is okay. A Godly man sustains his family, provides for their needs, and is faithful to God and his wife.
- Be a leader; be the head of your home. You must lead, provide, and protect.
- You have to willing to work hard to be a provider, a protector of your family (physically, emotionally, and spiritually), and protect her with the word of God.
- You have to nourish and care for your wife and show compassion toward her.
- Make time for your wife daily by talking to her, watching television together, reading together (books and the Bible), exercising together, and enjoying each other so that your marriage grows and is flourish with love, laughter, joy, and happiness. Be a good listener and allow your wife to help you.
- Allow the Holy Spirit to lead and control you instead of the influences of the world.
- Do not cheat, abuse, or disrespect, but be faithful, loving, honest, humble, patient, responsible, loyal, and devoted.

# To be a Godly father, you must:

- Forgive your father for being absent and choose to love him as God loves you.
- Lead by example. Be a leader by doing what is right toward your wife, your children, and others in your life.
- Teach your children the word of God, and teach them by the way you live your life and by how you treat others. Show them God's love by the way you love them.
- Spend quality time with your children and show them how love is an action.
- Love your children unconditionally, forgive them when they make mistakes, discipline them in love, and show interest in them and what makes them happy.
- Teach your children that no one is perfect, and we will all make mistakes, but we can choose to continue to grow spiritually. When you lose your temper and do wrong against your child, you must confess and repent to both God and your children.
- A Godly father is a man that children will feel honored to call "Dad."

Wow, Pops! That's deep! I know I will not be perfect, but I choose to go in the right direction. I want to be a Godly man, husband, and father. I want to be the Prince that every mother and father want their Princess to marry. I am going to be the man that God has called me to be.

The end

# Scriptures young Kings should know:

*Matthew 19:14   Jesus said, "Let the little children come to me, and do not hinder them, for the kingdom of heaven belongs to such as these."*

*Exodus 20:12 "Honor your father and mother, so that your days may be long in the land that the Lord your God is giving you.*

*Colossians 3:20 Children, obey your parents in everything, for this pleases to the Lord.*

*John 3:16 For God so loved the world that He gave His one and only Son, that everyone who believes in him should not perish but have everlasting life.*

*James 1:22 Be doers of the word, and not hearers only.  Otherwise, you are deceiving yourselves.*

*Proverbs 24:16 For though a righteous man may fall seven times, he still gets up; but the wicked stumble in bad times.*

*1 John 1:9 If we confess our sins, He is faithful and just to forgive us our sins and to cleanse us from all unrighteousness.*

*James 4:10 Humble yourself before the Lord and He will lift you up in honor.*

*Philippians 4:13 I can do all things through Christ who gives me strength.*

*Jeremiah 29:11 For I know the plans I have for you, declares the Lord, plans to prosper you and not to harm you, plans to give you hope and a future.*

*1 Samuel 16:7   For man sees the outward appearance, but the Lord sees the heart.*

*1 Corinthians 7:2 But because there is so much  sexual immorality, each man should have his own wife, and each woman her own husband.*

*Proverbs 18:22 He who finds a wife finds a good thing and obtains favor from the Lord.*

*Ephesians 5:23 For the husband is the head of the wife as Christ is the head of the church, His body, of which He is the Savior.*

*Ephesians 5:25 Husbands, love your wives, just as Christ loved the church and gave himself up for her.*

*Ephesians 5:28 In the same way, husbands ought to love their wives as their own bodies.  He who loves his wife loves himself.*

*Ephesians 5:31 "For this reason a man will leave his father and mother and be united to his wife and the two will become one flesh."*

*Ephesians 6:4 Fathers, do not provoke your children to anger; instead bring them up in the discipline and instruction of the Lord.*

*Proverbs 22:6 Train up a child in the way he should go, and when he is old he will not depart from it.*

www.ingramcontent.com/pod-product-compliance
Lightning Source LLC
Chambersburg PA
CBHW042118040426
42449CB00002B/87